THE AUREATE TROPHIES OF PROFIT & LOSS
(AND OTHER LYRICS FOR A COLD WORLD)

Stuart McPherson is a prize-winning poet and graphic artist whose work is influenced heavily by a lifelong involvement in the punk rock scene. His debut pamphlet, *Waterbearer* was published in December 2021, followed by the full-length *Obligate Carnivore* (Aug 2022) and *End Ceremonies* (Aug 2023), all via Broken Sleep Books. McPherson's poetry often grapples with masculinity, the survival of everyday life and political issues within late capitalist structures. His work has appeared in various journals and has been performed across the UK.

Also by Stuart McPherson

All Empty Vessels [with Aaron Kent]   (Broken Sleep Books, 2024)

End Ceremonies   (Broken Sleep Books, 2023)

Obligate Carnivore   (Broken Sleep Books, 2022)

Waterbearer   (Broken Sleep Books, 2021)

Pale Mnemonic   (Legitimate Snack, 2021)

CONTENTS

ISBN: 978-1-917617-92-5

Cover designed by Aaron Kent

Edited and Typeset by Aaron Kent

Broken Sleep Books Ltd
PO BOX 102
Llandysul
SA44 9BG

The Aureate Trophies of Profit & Loss

Stuart McPherson

Broken Sleep Books

It's all about bucks, kid. The rest is conversation.

— Gordon Gekko

ANTI-POEM

You are here and so is that rope. Not to advocate for it, but against it, like inverse policing or the way coordinated rocket launches might dislodge a guillotine sharpened by the ceiling of the sky. It is arguable if this is the best way to start a poem, but so too it can be argued that the best way to calculate waste is to watch hungry pigs wallowing frictionless in their own slurry. If this is outrage then let it be climbed inside, into the uneaten remnants by the butcher's block, the lungs, the heart. Many breaths have been stolen and so has our love. I'll send it to you in the form of an empty street full of fool's gold, or the light of a kitchen where knives in a drawer vibrate and feet drag across the laminate. If you thought a basement was the lowest place, then you've never stood upon a skyscraper, with its urinals and well-tailored suits. Ghosts, flesh, or figments of our imagination. To cast generalizations on the top percentile is a survival tactic learned by those who have lived in the grips of a vice, its mechanism, often observed by the wielder as *heavy metallic object,* is unilateral, or said differently from a tongue of specific tastes, is best used when tightened in one specific way.

SONG FOR OUR DESTRUCTION

Assessing human value is the same as measuring a mass of dead whales. Within their stomachs, the petri dish of our souls, we long for significance. It is a question of living and therefore a question of entrapment. Discard with ease the horror, or fashion it into crude, blunt instruments, something for trepanning in the name of both old and new scripture. Let it coalesce, centred in the palm; an electric knife or the succulence of plastic dripping into a fireplace made from neatly stacked coins. The dragging of a body onto tracks captures the golden moment, the glory of a fishhook lodged in the guts of those desperate to climb tall buildings, the clamour for morsels held in the beaks of birds greedier than those responsible for their crimes. Falling forward, lines become taut, and tarmac reddens into flash flood. Commuters unbeknownst lash out at all of the parts never seen, and ironically, this isn't how it should end, but that's the whole point. I hope gasoline fills up the emptiness and in unison we align, floating upwards to burn with phosphorescence, to become one again with the beauty of this earth sleeping so cosily in its stubborn pig-headed silence.

METHODOLOGY OF DISPATCH

It lurches, this malnourished place, our warm breath
damp against its tempered glass. Illegitimate symbols
    of prosperity fill the swamps where in deepest night
our pallid children set their feet. At Candlemas huddled
    between bricks, cherished items gripped with fervour,
paid for with subcutaneous fats, skin, chipped teeth, the
    music asphyxiated, drowned by a treble cleft asphalt
reflection. As taillights weep and fade, winter's viscosity
    falls quietly at the borders to all but the firm choke of
a young throat. *Home*. The word is mangled. A bloody
    incantation conjured from the glossy innards of nation
states so pudding thick and desperate for war business.

Within these midnight places of dispatch, a dove grips
a blade between its beak. Grass, a slip of yellowed plastic.
    A jacket daubed with the remnants of inner space or
a buoyant soul. And *still* impotent men button up them
    shirts. Damp earth to cover up Dante's hot mouth as
they chew the edge of Sunday's tender lamb. How deceit
    is reduced. *A governance of vampires is too crude* I said,
and evil can be grown in the blueish lamplight of each
    advantageous house, gardens strewn with wildflowers
ready to bloom, rhizomes hooked within an oesophagus.

GATHERED EXPRESSIONLESS MEN

Crepuscular in transference; calculated.
　　The way you linger. A charcoal seabed
dragging down our perfect light for the
　　　meticulous wringing of any living neck.

How you suck the marrow from baby pink
　　　limbs, smack your lips, lick fingers as
fat rivulets outwards; gravied blooms of
　　celestial expansion. Ball joints wrenched

from socket, both in relocation and abject
　　　terror. There you wait, sheet-like in the
treetops ready to blame a brisk wind for
　　the kidnap of every young, frail soul.

To bag them up. For slop poured under
　　　thrones, to extrapolate, heighten those
repugnant seats above desolate shop level
　　eyelines. Sweep up every single piece of

frailty pressed between the fingertips of

    parent and child. Drink dry the mother's

milk, imprison the fathers, eviscerate elderly

    relations atop tall pyres, observe from

country stables to warm the stud. Gallop fox

    fields with clubs dripping in rich garnet

ringlets. To be savoured, chewed, dropped

    dangling into the dulled beaks of fattened

birds who will never fly the nest or feel the air

    underneath wings. Shake loose gold coins,

shatter pottery with truncheon raps. Install

    ticketing on every spare inch of uncorrupted

natural beauty left unscorched. They stand in

    front of us, their raw cracked commissures.

Unholy mouths unable to contain the worming

    tentacles hidden beneath such velveteen cloth.

SATELLITE PARTY

Sit beneath a lapse of pulled cotton to watch with awe the gun metal so thoughtlessly hammered into spheres and thrown across a tortoiseshell of dusk and frog song. The littered sky staring down upon Athens corrupted with dry trees, hunted by orange flames. *This* laughter, that look of petulance flying in the face of instinct to claw at clock hands, to discard the camel alongside all its straws, the omnipresence of broken backs. Apparently, our blood shares the same state of liquidity, or so you say, but have you ever sacrificed yourself for the blueprint of a house that you can never really own? Expressions fill the silence of a blunt shape hung up by its fingernails, and despite the lush vegetation so beautiful and crooked, we procrastinate, argue about endgames. Calendars dampen unbeknownst, torn apart by pirouetting feet with no care to take unless solemnly read or spoken to in verbatim via a crumpled melancholy letter.

WISHLIST

Is this it? All this fuckery and terror?
    A tendonitis of broken news wanting

dark and inappropriate position, of
    bad omens or an exercise in ligature.

How you love to own that hot ache so
    deep within the offended muscles.

Except our arms aren't meant to be this
    twisted; right angled, odd limp insect.

We should be asleep now but there are
    choices to make between the draws

of long-shot fanaticism, or a life bereft
    of hope. That clouting fist on a door

is a precursor to necessary dignified rest,
    some basic standards of humanity.

All I ask is to feel the briefness of time,

    to avoid the shrapnel of snail shells.

Even still, I might ask the question of

    hunger, of what may happen without.

GOVERNANCE

Deadlock at slide three due to empirically false market
assumptions. Numbers skewed in midnight restlessness,
yet somehow falling for it before conscription to garbage
vessels at capacity. What is hierarchy but a series of failed
police officers getting their own back. *The bubbling under of
rage quotas. The bastardization of language.* List pricing limits
the ingestion of paint volumes necessary for spitting onto
canvas. How did you sleep last night? How are those kids?
You look so very pale. Maybe pivot via new on-trend social
platforms to enhance mummification ratios. Hyper-kudos
forces us to depart from weedkiller as model for effective
driveway management; adopt napalm, adopt anticlimax.
Are these interview techniques used to ensure skillset?
Pleasure as flame licks at the dandelion leaves. Think of a
brazen summer heat, think of grand plumages on fire and
pinballing around our tinder dry houses. In my absence,
find the lists which must be finished. My internal organs
are impeded. Is this pain carpel tunnel syndrome? See HR
response. See *meets expectations*, see genetic mutations, see
task embodiment, see executive level retreat. Salary sacrifice
schemes are withdrawn upon first cancer cell diagnosis.
Life's secret is discovered too late to make up the minutes.

VALUE

The whales are fighting back by launching themselves across the bow. But what to do? Throw ourselves across our desks? Parachute en-masse across horizontal cities to smother corporate foxholes? I've had many boring conversations about the subject and words have chopped tangible sentiment into driftwood. To float belly down on the Atlantic, the bowl of a fifty-foot wave topped with a white and grey fondant horse. Those dumb masters of echolocation, I can hear their songs, and I will find a boat of my own to sink, drag pale bodies down to that garbage reef where our treasured skeletons will sway in unison beneath their pyramids of vomited worthless currency.

APATHY CATALOGUE EXPLORATION

Dear garden full of stones and clay, I apologize for the neglect. I've watched young stalks rupture the surface of your soil, felt sunlight wrap around your body as attentive lover, as palliative care for neatness. All heatwaves are sent to break the wills of people too punch drunk to stand, or reclaim bricks stolen by the landlord's newest plot. Windows peer outward onto patchy lawns and lamplit driveways, our skins a striking strip for the sparks of a match. Good appetites are present and so is this grinning corpse. Remnants of the night sloshes in the bowl, ice cream as fuel for late-stage capitalist enterprise. You can't hear without sound, but still, we love to see the gore. We think about that old tree slouched out front, plant instead Rosaceae, its blossoms a clockwork all apple pink in the spring.

ARCHIPELAGO

All children are to be turned into tallow, and the remnants of our calendars are blunt as a pig's ear. There is a place where the water pools, desolate as religious words whispered into cracked ceilings. It bends iron, curls the crayon from wettened walls. We love our evaporated young; the way their bodies fold into the nostalgia of that very first shipping forecast. There's a foul mist that creeps in the wintertime, a whipped foam that bulges on the water. In the distance, a dog barks and all conversation turns to the smell of soot stinking from cracked chimney stacks. This bloody rage offset with bribery; a promise of stale bread cast from the hands of this year's best illusionists.

DRINKING FROM THE WELL OF ABSOLUTISM

Embrace disgorged tradition. Embrace unholy procession of

kingmakers draped in flagrant atrocity blankets. How easy

the stick breaks over common backs, how allegiance drips

from the rafters. Towers carved under duress congeal in non

consensual patterns. In the bloated lungs of corpses, lineage is

stolen, as is the land, as are seedlings stamped by horseshoe

into dry soil. Embrace collage of insipid media tactics. Inbred

tourist attractions grout the tiles of temporarily assembled

public urinals. Deliberately whitened streets are swept of all

synthetics. All non-conforming shapes suppressed, held

down by ink and gavel, robbed in broad daylight and brutally

beaten into transparency. Nearby, an exuberant nest. Its

hungry beaks are unable to know angles of a feather crushed

into hot tarmac. Compounded by engines, by long commute

or desolate traction. Horizontal dusk is swollen as a piss-ridden

bladder. Each clock hand passing into evening sends another

to the grave. Hail feasts for the boiled, for those that are set

upon. Agree to hold synchronised starvation tactics, avoidable

suicide as acceptable spectator sport. In lieu of slaves, the rich

sell off their families for a brief taste of luxurious black gold.

WHITE COLLAR LEAGUE TABLE EFFLUENT

Translucent figures command obedience to unknowns and tablatures certainly not welcome. Those caught contractually are motioned by the process as precious metals warp against curves and are dehydrated by the most precise machined edges. Political games are crushed between four walls, or excuse for missing salient points. The sound of broken news, of rapid cell multiplication, and such regretless pain devices are applied to squeeze with sheer violence the luminous sweet fluid. They climb the apple trees, pick ripened fruits left rotting in the orchard mulch, whilst scant pips are enveloped by our mother's arms and blessed by the sun to grow into something that *could be*, except though, for the chomping of high-rise psychopaths. All life is rubbed into uneven soil, the phone rings off the hook for spacious rooftop views across lush oasis of city populace.

SUBURBAN INSURANCE SCAM CASH-IN

I whisper into my ears that there is nothing left to hold.

Music plays quietly; all stooped postures are punished.

Life's privilege is raked into the cloying earth, giving

nourishment for crimson plants so selfish for the light.

Competition is boring. I'd rather be an everglade crocodile

waiting for a buoyant warm carcass to violently savage.

If the water is salted, maybe I can float. If I hold this metal,

maybe I can sink to the bottom; my father's bicycle did?

It is a project of deceit dressed as art. It's the constant nag

of a tail eager to be fussed. It is all those slogans we find

humming in our own rusted garbage cans. It's a feeling

that despite all of this knowledge you've been taken for

a fool. When books go rotten, the pretend ones always

reek the worst, the graduating stench of a lonely magpie.

ENGINEERING A MONOLITH

They ask us to keep the carcasses of trees within our
homes now hammered into bastardized lumber, and
designed for cavities requiring saturation with the

necessary volume of darkened neuromagnetic signal.
Dull winter lamplight sees the arrival of snow, which
sweeps up all the frail bodies and discards with ease

the hopefulness of spring as the shattered windows of
a town folding up an ice-cold kiss. It's chosen figurines
present to its people a cloud of origami butterflies that

flex before swarming from the snap of a gold cufflink.
It matters not how often we sing songs about holding
on, there is always the friction of a fingertip that lifts

thought out of mind and mind out of metal womb and
when I say womb, I mean nothing supplied with blood
nor spirit but a place pregnant with our desire to hoard

sickness aka all those cheap and meaningless trophies.
It becomes fact of life. The amputated forests cry out for
their children. All agents of change have been outfoxed.

THE DAY VENTURE CAPITALISTS REMOVED LIGHT
AS A FREE PUBLIC HEALTH BENEFIT

Transactions of the sun knotted into the coat of each family dog. How they pushed the orange rays through the wiry pelt, a brief warmth when pitched against windless repetitions of rotten oath, of ownership. To share in the apprehensive dusk of private garrisons trigger happy for bursts of sharp surprise. Even so, a wonderful peace in the going about of things, the settling down of a nesting dove. The breakage of a mirror helped into the stomach of a gulping litterbin. Laughter coalesced in gutters, cherished toys, our memories pushed around for loose change. *It faded to a pinhole as they dragged it away.* We monitored the temperature of our cooling bodies, talked of sea swimming, the silence of good food. The birds roosted in the chestnut trees; the air felt dense in its blue exaggeration. *'Moonless night'* I heard you whisper. The expression on her face never changed as we held each other in our fragile arms.

ATTACK ROUTE FROM EAST RIVER

Wall street under foot when risen
    from oily waters barely concealing
a barnacled back of scale to think
    that none would be a slave to it.

Trading weapons lightly dusted
    by beaten mothwing choking up
the mechanisms of a gun barrel so
    cognisant of risk against the *ROI*

of flattened corporate sausage
    making factories. Arrogant bodies
in the district throw rolls of paper
    to curtail the rumbling of ancient

monsters as bribery, as cheapest
    deterrent to avoid the dismantling
of competitive modern office chair
    hierarchies. Without recompense

upon horizon, treading soil to write

    urban obituaries, a three headed

king comes again to reclaim what is

    rightfully ours as made by hand.

Recharge then these minority units.

    Scorch all battalions of lower to

middle tier management org charts

    and have them tremble at the depth

of massive imprints. The sheer

    heat of radiation belched around

the serrations of gargantuan pointed

    teeth readied to gnaw on each

laborious process is not enough.

    To be sure all magnificent beasts

are unified in absolute destruction.

    Rise up to save us from ourselves.

DISCUSSION #1

Hi yeah, it's good to know, good for you to know that I crushed my own trachea to adjust the tonality, it helps me talk to you and it's good to know your levels of commitment. Don't you care about this? We're offering you a way to smash through the glass ceiling of mediocrity, envelope the welcome blessings of those expressionless men. Good to know that we forgot about the inconvenience of your broken heart, you'd be easy to move with the ball of my foot in your back. Good to know you wept in front of your family, what must they have thought? *weakness.* Good to know you're weak because pain is strength and we'll be happy to give you more opportunity to juggle chainsaws, what's your preferred method? We are mandating the blood eagle. Good to know you're able to attend for once because we need to talk to you about something very serious, yes, the earth is burning, but you're not maintaining a sustained upwards trajectory. We constructed lodgings in that impoverished place because we genuinely do care, just look at the social engagement. Good to know your thoughts, we really enjoyed the one where that projectile loosened your skull. The look on their faces! Everyone applauded and it's great to see you bringing your true self to the table. We'll make a note of it for discussion. It's good to know that you can be honest, and we saw how you spilled all that dark matter from your mouth. Please know that all ideations on black hole theory are not to be shared publicly. Hi, yeah are you free? We need you to clean those coagulations from your local environment before this information goes out. This year our mantra has been vetted by a third party, they've told us to own three pillars, I'm sure that they will resonate? They look the same as *mutilate, destroy, kill.*

MIGRATING FROM AN OPEN WINDOW

A square of down just wanting to rest its bitten
corners and moistened for the chewing palette.

Enduring sleep, a body floats atop its own black
lake as fuel to halt the moons silver sword or the

dullness of an egg tooth tapping its way across an
abstraction of murdered night. To be lost amidst

adolescence, slipped between the pages of a book
written for silhouettes of a future self. Symbioses

held gently as an orb, as proof of the hatching of
another life worth living, not the black carbon of

a birdwing. All freedom is reduced to dust as we
rise up from cracked palms to escape into the sun.

BINGE WATCHING DOCUMENTARIES THAT DISCUSS EVENT HORIZON AS AVOIDABLE POLITICAL CONSTRUCT

Unpopular opinion brines in the apple bowl, stagnates
with penicillin myth. Wasp circulations: an ageing populate.
Lines of ants navigate garden waste disposal systems.

After tax, the opening of our veins into Edwardian sockets
to thicken the fuse wire. A belching up of well cared for
lawn debris in the shadow of properties so purposefully

enabled to buckle under solar rage. Hydration is quick
to parch beneath subsidence or polemic mismanagement.
They calculate our death, see our shallow roots wither.

The relief of demographics, of elderly statesmen residing in
that sweet spot where the enshrined ransacking of every
final pleasure fills the vaults. This inheritance racket neatly

implemented as necessary freshwater spring protection.
Know the smoking out of worker bees, the taste of down-
pressed insecticide manipulates. On knees we crouch to

find modicums of transparency, any lingering lung inhalant.

We sit on the precipice of sunsets, drained of orange, red, of romantic meaning, just the bleach of pale magnolia tinged

purple. The radiance of bright extinction, *hand them your children*. They gather their own, enroll their names into the middle tier management of climate crisis research teams.

THE COMPANY MASCOT

A bluebird lands upon an old town church, watches over those left alive. Observing from a feathered head, it paints over existence, over mind, the way aged red meat becomes striated, marbled fat, dotted blue. Blue trees cowed above the water's edge: their limbs dipped in a littered creep of violence. From the bankside, a goading of helpless pups, each litter labelled 'remnant'. All office buildings huddle in their counsel, and circulars are chewed before the envelope. On the lanyards of workers hangs the truth. Blue lips search for air, for remedy minus taxation. Mars is wrangled by an ogrish sky. A silhouette for every newborn bricked inside a spore ridden home, as above lands the bird, the governance of its beak. Its feathers are unruffled now, quite content with knowing that all capitulations have been daubed with blue.

FORTITUDE

The sun rises, the sun sets, and bridges between horizontal thumb and forefinger spread to furrowed temples, creak as a ships deck might creak with music of financial plenitude, the prison state of six Georgian walls, some insulated wallpaper dead set against fire safety regulations. Unable to be inspected by any caring 'would be' counsellors, all ready to shift blame towards the charred skeletons of a night shift worker effervescent in the evening air and measured against distinct limbic odours. How smoking skin and bone can be compared to all recent contemporary benchmarks, the modern standards of *other* tabulated historical data, its value rising up to fall on the knife edge of a bat wing, the moon a circular saw jammed into the cold midnight of every father sat with his only desolate child, as the ground falls away, rumbles as loud as a preschool stomach sucking in the notion of existence or satiation as a very serious happiness. And all the while they are hatchet faced; all the while happy to drop coins into palms, the trash talk of twin cymbals kissing in our orchestra of senescent light.

IN THE MIDNIGHT OF A FANTASY RESIGNATION LETTER

I open a window to the garden and embrace its edges, think about the existence of helpless shadows even in the nicest places; an impotent vessel lashed against a harbour wall, a lame dog in an alley. It's my favourite thing, laying here, thinking about all the things I could have been. All the places I could reach down to touch, soil damp and musty between finger and thumb. I push the glass to let in the cold. I'm not young, not old just a limbic state of something in between, something held between the gentle lips of dawn, a worker bee in spring, a pavement ant. The trees are all talking about how slow I am and they're right. I never used to be this slow. The air is cool across my chest; the stars are out. Such soundless absence but for the distant draw of an engine. I hear the waves lapping at the bow, the labradors ribs, the skip of its feet. The boat groans as it folds itself into the deep blue pelagic.

MOMENTS BETWEEN VALUELESS MEETINGS AS CATALYST FOR ASTRAL PROJECTION

Six brittle legs and two folded wings tangled up in silk. Daydreams so far from hyperbole, the idle stare of a dead eyed lens. To the soothing squalls of water whipped between rooftops, the importance of stepping outside this slouched heap. *You* towards *me*; *me* away from my own shape. Far from grades, structural tests, bell curves so ignorant of the exponential increase in forest fires. More discarded fuel or the carbon of lost souls' ground into dust as recommended, *as optimized*. All third-party output is just office layout as heinous political joke. We sit upon the bluey snow, feel the breaking at the caps. A ticker tape parade of Borealis or the start of the Sargasso Sea where eels swim between minutes as illustrative depiction of a powerful, simple thing, the crude materials from which dense mountains are carved. We travel forward, *Clueless*, willed on by vice, the smack of lips upon exotic fruits, lemons, emerald limes, although there is love. Impossible to lose, it is foraged from the shod skin of ghostly winking stars that once we laid beneath, bobbing. Caught between icebergs, incisors, molars, the cruel mirror of our moon. How letting go brings us back from abject corrosiveness. We are sitting so still.

MEDIA STAGED CAFETERIA INCIDENT

Sky blue clothes or condescending sweater.
Index pinched plate, oil crisped bacon bits.

Business talk convoluted as to wade across
foul water spate rivers. *Oh, Hadron Collider!*

To crush souls is so deliciously photogenic.
Brylcreem hair occluded by plastic barrier.

A hot plate barricade, *such fierce competition.*
Who is grubby, most premeditated behind

the lens's bulging node. A bioluminescent
gland of egg. Sun yellow; gelatinous image

poached in a well-seasoned pan. *Spooned
over.* Swilled around high smoking point of

saturated fat. That after platitudes: wonder-
ment. Of conversant leather interiors heated

up. A bulletproof vehicle quick to escape the
pungencies of sugary food, cheap soft bread.

OH, GLORIOUS BLOODSPORT

Helplessness as fingers rasped along pearlescent
scales, *to fillet*. Small bodies silvering between
stones, long lipped under daylight, a promise of
nourishing things. The mouth appeal of fluorescent
flies, barbs pushed through skin. To be hit by shoe,
by shovel. Gasping at the language of our dreams
frothing from the guts, all glassy eyed & cataract
resplendent. *We begin to rattle.* They line the banks
in silhouette, fingers flaring out the gills as bones
are crushed & bowed by heel. The soft shoal flickers
into an eyelid, the lines sink as we lay before the sun
in the shadow of our death. *Such prosperous laughter.*
They cast their hook baits through the slovenly air.

RED MEAT ISSUE

Boats are red and fleshy as ridden.

    Black water to red, frothed by tooth,

        by hand, by pernicious intellect.

    Stony beaches, a cold shingle so

obtuse it clatters across the white cliffs.

    Red livers glossed in morning light,

        as risen dough, as bitten tongue.

    Of red seeping out of creases from an

indiscriminate raft sent from wound.

    Suffused, a fulsome red, red mothers

        and fathers holding thornless stems.

    Roses wettened and absent of colour.

Red carpets, silk ties. Sewage paper or

    tabloid hammered fists. Torrid faces

        wrinkled, set alight as burnt hands

    wrench raw forearm of sky, as witness.

We repeat, we repeat, *we repeat,* and all the

    while sustenance is syphoned through

a hose until midnight streets are lined

    with anaemic bodies. We stretch out

        in expanse, sat atop a puerile vomit

    of distraction, a vented red rage, pointed

finger of blame. All stars will collapse

and in the forests of our twin earth red

wolves howl at a crimson moon.

It fills with gleeful manipulation. Thick

slabs of someone once defined as water or

someone badly misrepresented pooled

in-between an infantile and arbitrary

definition. Bordered land; *home bodies*.

Faces on alert, red as enemy. Online recipe

search; how meat is easy to marinade, to

cook over hot coals. Crudely stripped

and loosened against our will. A blood

orange anchored in the depths is a red heart

sobbing to be kindly placed back inside the

vessel that it didn't ask to be born into.

RESENTMENT AS UNWELCOME HOST

There is nothing to show for it, no utopic ideation, nor the hyper realism of joy minus re-entry. Without plateau or the safety of frosted glass blurring our death in the witching hour of every known end. Contented living creatures creep so fearlessly in sleep same as that which cannot be defined pushed outwards between pale gaps familiar with the chew of each nourishing meal. Laughing at the sky, lacrimal ducts are a bad liar and bruised to roll with each corporate punch. There is nothing to show but the paperwork, the whipping of skin as minutes flay the back. Late night shop antics to limit the speed of each working week. Salt in the wounds, vinegar in the eyes, bloodied moonlight a mirage of black ice to slip across same as a cheap length of fabric. A longevity of synthetics or poor lumber support. It floats above it obstinately, the waste, the foaming scum. Productivity assessment is a mini party-political broadcast, a direct contrast to what is in the cupboards. Some claim expenses, others expire in the ironic benevolence of those who exude public best interests. Fingers are cupped around seven occipital crests. We drown beneath the bows of exclusive tethered vessels.

SUBMITTING AN ANNUAL LEAVE REQUEST

Little beaks sing winter songs in summer.
    All angular feathered heads look to the East.

To the mottled turquoise of daydreams and
    salient protagonists, an old tree holds no life.

As a skeletal hand, *it hurts,* and I can smell
    myself, headlines smothering like a pillbox.

Negative gains, a dagger in the earth's edge.
    Our cars are emptied, thirsting, cobwebbed.

A smorgasbord of moot points and famished
    cuticles: my nails bitter when chewed upon.

Needles of keratin are a pleasure between
    pincers; shrill notifications muting birdsong.

The colour green is a myth, unable to overcome
    the delicious twisting out of glum dollies of

chest hair: how did it come to this? All clothes
    froth from plastic bags too frail to hold them.

THINGS HAVE NEVER BEEN BETTER

wrestle sleep inside shallow graves resplendent   with inkblot
expression fluid   false everglades squeezed from twisted
humidities of inert working weeks where *we*   as poorly worn
imitation crocodile handbags   are flooded with midnight
serenities   of moons and stars   of winter fog spilled from the
mouths of grey shapes that in turn remove all unnecessary power
fluctuation dualities   a crepuscular meditation pose for each
permanent corporate idealist   as the foetal positions of parent
and child   as shadowy memoire nailed to the backs
of sleeping lions   morning coffees   weekend mindfulness as
formalised nature prescription   failures of each career
ladder a waterfall of rungs for us to bathe beneath   continue
to search for problems that we are told to own   to fix by the
gaslight of simple internal narrative as in   *adjust poor attitude*

ZERO WASTE MANIFESTO COMMITMENT

Work is important to us, so hoist a felled deer across your back. It will spill its lifeblood and that is meaningful. How we build a structure from all weight bearing dead animals, *pangolin, ostrich, iguana.* Your discontent is a problem for you to solve. In ablutions, cleanse yourself both outside and in. Those limp feelings are a hog halved and tied by hoof. Iced water spattering its diamond clouds refracted from hollowed ribcage. *Poor attitudes are bred by the heart.* Yours is flatlining, lazy as cider apples piled up to rot in some unpleasant orchard. Visit the bleached slaughterhouse, observe the laughing knives. Ghosts escape from windows and we will catch them by their transparent edges, assess them, put them to task until all souls fill our pockets. Deliberate currencies are cloaked, hidden beneath the heavy tan of roebuck pelt. Everything priceless pinched by membranous walls is rinsed out in a chemical bath.

EXPOSÉ

Fed without warmth or nutritious blue fruits crushed
    underfoot, dark as alveoli. Busy hands root through
fleshy bags of naïve souls, *the most vulnerable first*. An insipid
    blackness burns in the corners, as crime, as lamplight.

Through milky eyes, pencils scratch the matte of cheap
    paper. Don't cook, or wash genitals, or scrape the floral
blooms from your children's skin. *This heating is a luxury.*
    Its rusted underbelly is the landlord's speeding vehicle.

To feign collision, fake impact and its resulting insurance
    claim, detail infinitely how we all suffer, except of course
those with cold currencies, the bandwidths crudely stuffed
    into paltry bedding, between the edges of a skyscraper

or behind neon signs, under fingernails where it gathers
    into undead entities never able to haunt with any real
meaningful spectral luminosity. Never to wreak terror in
    the cavities of those who eat heartily, sleep under heavy

blankets. The feeling is one of sand falling through fingers,
    fists clenched by a solar vengeance. Ragged street cats
strip the carcasses of brittle bodies glowing in luminescence.
    We are saturated with the boundless positivity of such

excellent fortune. All these wholesome and compassionate

people living on such wonderful islands. To raise anchor,

sail away into the half-life of cheaply poured concrete. Our

disgust is a tail wagging in the comfortable quarters of

a spacious home with expensive floors and fittings. We talk

about *that holiday in France*. A mirage of petroleum, the

way shattered glass is a xylophone, the crunch underfoot

akin to first snow as rage bristled by the *Arc de Triomphe*.

We sit, romanticise the prospect of swooping under convex

shields, catching rubber bullets between our bright white

teeth. What cinema! *Francis Ford Coppola, Oliver Stone*. Crumbs

from tonight's food choke in their own viscous amalgam.

Our idle feet sit propped upon their bruised heads as voices

gather in the branches. The limes line the streets, spores

linger in the slums, and we wait for them to grow into dense

shadow, the one that eats our young in urban legend.

ON THE DAY CAME THE CALL

It rippled through the air and all monarch butterflies paused atop flowerheads. In her face the truth, and so in his, whilst outside the day syncopated its knocking rhythms and cars sucked on bitter fuel for forward movement. Suburban letterboxes fish hooked, cut open at the corners. Fields already stripped bare readied their furrows whilst in the weight of silence he sat, thoughtless, skin pixelated and rising off the bone. How everything continued. Shock and awe infective as antidote for wide eyes. The non-believers baulked, and the rest wrapped themselves in knowledge of efficiencies, of digital media as heavy cloak of self-identity, of true transformation. Did they ring the bell at the stock exchange today? The clouds looked different, and I pressed against the ceilings cornice. What to do but fill the lungs with a new type of breath and tip oneself into the archives of the deceased. How easy it might be to slip into a new suit, wake up in a trench only to have a chest partitioned by shrapnel. It's a comfort really, knowing that everything ends, and so pleasurable to hold onto such melodramatic tangents. Once in a century magic has no anti-climax, except for the ignorance of it, the expectation, the publicly owned routes to find meaningful return in exchange for quick, unnoticeable blemish. What weightlessness before the ever presence of a shop floor, the artificial notes deleted, the wrangling as callous performance ritual, and the sickly messages of self-protection and the endless freedoms of the universe as entered into through the frayed neck of a cut rope.

THE AUREATE TROPHIES OF PROFIT & LOSS

At one time, all babies were born as feathers
and half the weight they should have been.
Refuse sacks lay sweltering in the sun,
the stench of industries' backwards wet
dream. Politicians unprepared pushed them
through gaps to hide them. All resolution
did was float us up into the hot, stinking air.

*

I am jealous of first memories, nostalgic
platitudes, and warm conversation. Take
me back to that glassy ford and let its cold-
water wash all over me. In the heat of
summer, they lift me out to dry. I watch my
future self drowning inside the behemoth
tombs of wretched 1960's architectural bliss.

*

The festive season is the most fertile
place to pre-seed the benefits of wealth
division. Santa Claus is an agent of the
state. I remember the night he removed
all childhood magic from our ears with a
drinking straw. That year our fairy lights
vibrated, a precursor to vivid electrical fires.

*

I enjoyed hurting myself, the adrenaline
of it. A pickaxe in the fontanelle, to fall
willingly from roof to ground. Parental
concern makes you feel so much love.
Nowadays I must consider optics and
whether or not it violates the employee code
of conduct. Nobody likes a risk assessment.

*

After work he would sit in his chair and eat
shadows from a bowl. He never really said
that much. He cycled to the city every day.
He thought rules were absurd. He was a
biochemist and instrumental in developing
painkillers. He experienced spooky action
at a distance without ever really knowing it.

*

The primary school teacher was impressed
by my story about rats despite the plagiarism.
He applauded the graphic nature of it,
the teeth biting through flesh and bone. I
won a prize. The other children seemed
afraid. At home I watched films where
people got shot in the chest, the face.

*

As a child I dreamt of building rocket ships born from the dead carcasses of bedroom furniture. When they came to collect the weekly rubbish, they took both the furniture and my dreams. I was left with no apology. If things were different, I would have taken off and nuked this total shitshow from orbit.

*

They surrounded her and tore open her clothes. I sat in the sandpit and tried not to look. The sun was hot. The boys laughed. Was I a boy or a girl? The sun was hot, and the grass no longer grew. The quarry seagulls unfurled their wings. The sun was hot, the sky up above a beautiful topaz blue.

*

I never understood the complexities of admiration. Later on, I would try to unravel the knots. The way the owner of the book told his boss to go fuck himself, and then left to live off the land. By definition a bad father, he threatened politicians with violence through defiant physical attributes.

*

When they kicked my dog to death his little rubies of blood scattered across the floor. I put them in my pocket to keep them safe. All office coffee machines accept them as valid currency. They're uncomfortable to carry though, especially in ill-fitting trousers. Hexagonal edges rub against skin.

*

To stop being beaten I had to lie. There were worms all over the curtains and none left for the snake. I hadn't let them out, but her hands made my ears ring. A useful lesson then, in compliance. I've had so many bosses over the years, so many reptiles to feed. Telling the truth is a dangerous game.

*

When she married again, I protested by throwing up peanuts all over the interior of a sleeping bag. It didn't stop them, and they didn't stop buying peanuts. Some battles are impossible to win, and little people are easy to ignore. My last boss asked why my drawers contained bar snacks and a pillow.

*

The entire world wants you to lose heart early. The more pieces you lose, the more room there is for goals, motivational speeches and the acceptance of sub median pay grades. I lost mine when he came home from work to snatch away my food. Now I always feel hungry, even though I've eaten.

*

Election and he spent the morning weeping. The cursed earth tilted on its axis. They rescinded gravity, lashed coronal ejaculations to the ankles of the poor. Police officers became virulent with excessive rage. Killing animals became more popular than ever, as did all luxurious pipe tobacco.

*

How do you enter friendship groups if you don't relate? Those newly built houses always had such lovely symmetry, a garden gate, some red peonies, a driveway. Living off cold concrete floors will mutate you into a different breed of social creature. Eating baby food for satiation sharpens the tongue.

*

Living in a council house. Living in a big unaffordable house. Downsizing. Living in a medium sized modern three bed. Living unsustainably in a ribcage dressed up as restoration. Living in a house with no heat. Each one can have a room where lessons on authoritarianism are taught so very quietly.

*

The policeman wouldn't let me look at my bike when he asked me to describe it. When they delivered *those videos* to my house it was fine though, and they smiled. The policewoman taking notes was nice, but she didn't explain how for malnourished kids' society dampens down all future appetites.

*

It's exciting to miss school so your parents can work. Whenever this happened, I would place a small drop of potion under my tongue. I grew in size, yes, but after a while my eyes kept falling out. They rolled into a pile of receipts and set them alight. The resulting smoke reeked of saturated fat.

*

Advocates for domestic violence sought to raise funds via venture capitalists. It was a new technology. They would build a cloaking device into the damp proofing of every house thus enabling monsters to rule the world. No one knows if they succeeded. The initial tests were on the abject, the poor.

*

She met a new guy. He arrived by plane but when it came to departure, he had to take Prozac before climbing into the cockpit. His career had been in the forces, but his passion was cookery. They would settle their arguments by seeing who could create the tastiest dish conceived from the offal of cat.

*

Calendars were blasphemous and never ever allowed. So I missed that it was a new year, and my old trousers didn't fit and everyone stared at my ankles. They didn't hear the clicking of the device strapped to my chest. Every month I added a new stick, a new fuse wire to send them all to hell with.

*

No-one explains what you are working towards, and economics is another name for hand-to-hand combat. You need a sharp blade in order to progress. They won't let you in unless they see potential. If you can prove that you have killed your own soul, they will award you the very best of grades.

*

Commercial enterprise makes for successful youth. Bar work, factory work, loading production lines from the foothills of a seasonal opportunity. Modelled on lessons learnt and handed down from parent to child. You're nearly there, everything is on track, those beige cubicles are ready for you.

*

True discipline is a pair of fluorescent trainers. Fuck the health benefits of running, this is about medals. This is what the world wants. The best houses on the street would make *a whooshing* sound when all that metal would come spilling out of the front door. It was absurd that he made me do the training.

*

I found out that innocence is not a precious metal, but a plastic. Most of it can be found floating in oceanic garbage heaps. The media always covers it up. My teenage conquests went to the edge of the water, made boats from pornographic magazines, our bodies silhouetted as we lit them on fire.

*

One night I worked the bar of a special event. They asked for some strippers who fucked the men right there on the floor. A naked guy walked up and ordered a diet coke. Before I was told to remove the used condoms from the toilets, my boss talked to me about how I would be emergency taxed.

*

The breakdown of our relationship and my broken arm were connected by astrological conspiracy. The tail of Hale-Bopp infected me with jealousy and the wheels of my skateboard with inertia. In bed, I wore the coat she gave me. No medical attention. I soaked my arm in Witch Hazel as I grieved.

*

The way to pay off your credit card debt is to punch a hole in the ATM. However, if you're too anxious to commit crime hide in the foyer of a bank dressed up as a lime tree. On paper, you're a risk. At night, you're the reason why they celebrate. A cocktail recipe in the dregs of a gutter used for spitting into.

*

I wanted to breathe so I ran as far away as possible. Unfortunate then, that in the absence of pressure all the weather systems in my skull started to ooze. I became a rain cloud, El Niño, a thermohaline circulation. All the lecturers purporting freedom of expression got punished, regularly berated.

*

Losing your virginity can be a dead end. Mine got caught in a noose and the law said it was a glitch. To accelerate towards love is to throw your skeletal remains into a black hole. It rattles the seabed pearls cupped by a clam. Your past lovers don't see the blunt knife of moonlight that shucked them loose.

*

During elections he told me how he wept, how his tears fell upon the ground to spew forth roses, sweet strawberries. The earth was still and for a moment all humanity fell silent, hypnotized by the beautiful omnipotence of a blackbird song. Sunflowers turned in hope towards the sky.

*

Despite owning many houses and a volume of fraudulent shares he wouldn't give me any money for food. He said I needed to learn lessons in value. In an act of goodwill, he sent sea kelp just in case a nuclear reactor was compromised, and I needed to flush out all the radiation coursing through my veins.

*

The bank called me in. They had concerns about my purchases. They pulled up a screen and played video footage of executions and automobile fatalities. I explained that I needed to buy glasses and books. They jangled car keys in front of my face, talked about machetes against a throat.

*

I sat on a hillside and released bluebottles from my mouth. I chose this spot because of the melancholy of watching distant traffic, a haze of garnet taillights. Although cathartic, there was no audience. The flies landed on my skin, flew me back to a tiny room. Their king told me that I would never be believed.

*

She had a boyfriend, so we slept together without having sex. Every night the hidden monologue from Robbie Williams' debut album would wake me up. One night she woke up too and I confessed to her that I had murdered myself and she needed to call the police. Years later she did. I thanked her.

*

Post-study I was trapped within a snow globe. I made some calls, cycled ten miles a day to load cat food onto a conveyor belt. You could smell the maggots when you got a bad pallet. When they shook it, I had to give them all my wages plus a book on identity penned by Lord Anthony Giddens.

*

After I got a degree, I worked a job laying basketball courts. After this, I got a job collecting debt. It was strange to me, having to wear a tie. There were reports that showed the team leader how many minutes you were late. It's a vibe that after everything you are destined to live this way.

*

When I told my mother about what had happened, she cried. When I saw her again she wouldn't look at me. And after that I couldn't get in and she left a dead crow outside in one of my shoes. The house was then folded away with a note that said "I just can't remember letting him touch you"

*

During the summer I rented a cardboard house. Above the door hung five spiders and a family of flies. I slept on the deathbed of the woman who owned it before. I lay next to her for six months before they told me she was there. I wonder if she saw my posters, my books, my pale round stomach.

*

Living is fun until you realise you've been forgotten. Standing at the end of pier choosing between the sun and the sea. The curdled promises of youth and all the world's oysters wedged between its pages. Where to go from here? To become an aux cable hoping that someone will plug you in?

*

I went to see a career advisor and they expressed surprise. This advice was usually reserved for the malleable. They offered me some leaflets, one on the largest items ever to be crushed by a hydraulic press, the other on angler fish and how saltwater exposure can help humans with the evolution of gills.

*

He was in charge of contempt and used his brown suit to amplify it. The keys to the school jangled in his pocket, a brittle octopus. We loaded up the mincemeat machines and he came out to tell us about our mistakes. We laughed at him, and he agitated in the rearview mirror as we drove.

*

That first one is a fucker. You're not used to nodding and smiling so much. Incredible how they make you hang up all of your clothes before swiping in. The rules float around in jars that they lift up to your lips. It reminded me of when I was forced to watch an anaconda constrict that baby goat.

*

The boredom was so intense my nose bled. Technically, it's called a spider phone they said before huddling around it in their suits. From the speakers came orchestral music. They all took notes, whilst one by one their bones splintered noisily as garden canes. I felt so temporary, a limp frame bent in two.

*

Before the financial crash we enjoyed the handmade chocolates, thought about what to decant into crystal. I tried my hardest to keep myself from astral projecting, but my aura kept erupting from my mouth. They demanded I tell them everything that I knew about the Northern Lights. *Everything.*

*

Satanic rituals were very widespread. One Christmas the cult leader returned to fetch her underwear lost beneath his desk. They were tangled in a headset still connected to a customer. On his command, we all had to be draped in cold human skin, a way to urgently adjust key performance indicators.

*

Someone was shitting all over the toilets on purpose. They made us wait in the cubical to try and see. We never found them, although we did see three foxes, an ostrich and a Komodo Dragon. I put out my hand and got bitten, hallucinated about crashing into the side of a phosphorescent mountain.

*

They paid me in Kola nuts. I always had to leave a handful on the doorstep for someone I couldn't see. We lived upstairs and I sanded the floorboards with a toothbrush. Dust got everywhere. I went to the dentist, and he told me all my teeth were dirty, that payment for the treatment equals Kola nuts.

*

The second one was located below a concrete tower. The training consisted of mathematics and target practice with small bore rifles. There was pride in not taking lunch. I always took mine and it angered them. The leader sat all alone whittling the limbs of ex-employees with a zombie knife.

*

General election, and he was weeping. He bought weapons and made man traps. A parliament of owls gathered. He cashed in all his assets, made shady deals and fueled his car with red diesel. He pushed seeds into the soil, bought in hay for the lamb of god and prepared for end times, the apocalypse.

*

The third one was a gift although the owner told me that employees not working their hardest were taking food from out of his children's mouths. He made a point of having his sports car washed in front of them for good motivation, to plead the case for consistently working fingers to the bone.

*

After our daughter was born, it snowed every night for a year. It wasn't her fault; I was struggling to pay the bills, and the bank had sent in the chem trail folks. One summer day, it settled so much that I froze to my desk. At this point they decided to enforce a strict new professional dress code.

*

Government compensation schemes are available for victims of crime. I had to fill out the form using mind tricks and under the light of full moon. They said I couldn't qualify because they wanted to keep all the money for themselves. I hacked off a pound of my flesh, sent it off to their appeals team.

*

Every morning a tall man would come and sit by my side before vomiting into my lap. He said that this was for my own personal development. We met again, and I had to talk through its consistency, what I thought he'd had for dinner the night before. *Fillet Steak*, he said…*you lot don't eat steak, do you?*

*

The embarrassment of being found in a completely dissociative state. Someone took me into the room where they fired people. I can't remember going home, but when I returned, I dressed as Michael Myers so that everyone would be too afraid to talk about all the wild tropical countries they'd visited.

*

They decided to detach the country from the seabed. Illegal backhand tenders allowed them to build and attach multiple speedboat motors. With a shove, we all floated out into the sea before a helicopter flew down and airlifted away the most insistent politicians. The motors failed. We didn't have any food.

*

I felt my heart stop. Dizzy and sweating I fell down. *This is because you had to help them leave, isn't it.* I nodded and shed all of my hair. A swarm of little children came over to help sweep it under the carpet. I was surprised that no one noticed them, or the pale transparent ghost holding out its hand.

*

A machine scans people to see their career history. It passed a laser through my flesh and spat out some paper. It had a clown's face on it and read *why the fuck are you still here, you fucking loser*. I applied some face paint and attached a red nose. The next scan said exactly the same thing and we laughed.

*

They said that if we did things properly, it would be for everyone's benefit. The money would fall in, and humanity would be renewed. No one saw how big the shareholders had become. They were picking people up off the street and biting them in half, swallowing them, no chewing.

*

Sometimes people talk in entanglements. When they do it accelerates the human race towards their death. Just a flavorful word salad but *so necessary* for better employee relations. Or is it just an acupuncture needle pushed into muscle at the utterance of a consonant, the incontinence of every vowel.

*

The fourth one is still unknown. Things are different because someone has switched on all the appliances. To succeed you have to be able to transcend human form and become the spirit bird of capitalism, show a veracious nature, be cuckoo-like at rolling out all those tasty eggs, *but not too efficiently.*

*

They trialed operating the world as a bonfire. They sold tickets, including a VIP tier, a corporate box. It was warm and comforting, but when there were no more branches to burn the execs worried about their return on investment. They lied, told us that it wasn't a bonfire, blamed the trees.

*

Who needs to go outside anymore, we have all we need. The biggest corporations deem two things necessary, aspiration and high fructose corn syrup. All sports channels will eventually be replaced with continuous plastic surgery procedures. Envy and vitriol will become the highest rated pay-per-view.

*

This new trend of 30-minute makeovers has gone too far. The host is a landlord, and he sprays the property with spores instead of paint. At the end of the show, they make the mothers place their children next to the unfolding darkness. If they die slowly and unnoticed then it's a clear economic success.

*

Apparently, I'm not allowed to live stream my own demise on social media. It makes everyone look bad, especially in May. Why couldn't I have done it in the Wintertime when it could at least be attributed to the bad weather? It's not a good look, it puts our revenues at risk. *See page 37 of the new policy.*

*

Ultimately, we should blame the numbers. We've been trying to hit them for years. They sit behind everything. From the aureate trophies of profit & loss to the statements of exploited sex workers. How many pre-suicide text messages did you get? How many words, sentences, methods.

*

I opened up a tin of alphabet spaghetti and poured it onto a plate. The words seemed to suggest that if I didn't want to become the best version of myself that I should leave. I ate it all up and it had no impact on my muscles whatsoever. I pulled on a t-shirt that read "I am *so* the best" and left anyway.

*

They attached a radio to my ears and house bricks to my belt. They pushed me in, and I sank heavy as an anvil. To be considered financially viable, I had to swim to the surface as quickly as possible. All the while they shouted and pissed blood into the pool. They told the lifeguard that it was my fault.

*

Sleepless bodies rot better. I have already prepared by wrapping myself in a sheet. Only when the birds sing am I able to drift off, but until then a man wearing a different watch sits and rifles through my wallet. My face is a critique of its own poor complexion. I am assigned thoughtless merit quadrants.

*

I once touched a tree to feel a connection to the earth. Now it's bleached, eaten away by nature, the life's work of a family who toil at every given hour. A truck stops. He asks me if I want him to take it away for a fair price. We share in exhaustion by hanging from our faces gut encrusted fishing hooks.

*

A rhythm beating in the chest is so ectopic it exceeds all known safety thresholds. It makes me consider the levels of pollutant exposure or what was trending in the office. When I told her my health was at stake he didn't even turn around. It skips again, but he is more worried about my autosignature.

*

To escape from structure, I ran a race to see how fast a shape could be changed. It lasted a few years until the pandemic leveraged a crowbar beneath my ribs. The trickery of it. Those wily execs and their panopticons. Now I'm eating more than ever. On paper I'm productive but my clothes no longer fit.

*

I know I have to participate, but really, what happens if I don't? This was not the right response, and I had to make amends by setting up a table and a webcam. Every donation would result in me hitting my own hands with a hammer and offering up whimsical chat about B2B sales techniques.

*

I always said that I'd be completely present for my family. Funny then, that vampirism keeps a roof over our head. She pushes her fingers beneath my coffin lid, lifts it, asks if I want to come downstairs. I am a thick fog beneath the door. I ask her about her day before orchestral sounds summon me back.

*

Summer would sit deep in the stomach, the springtime in the head. Autumn's romance of future seasons, the winter in its reverence. They are algorithmic, blunted. Talking about the eclipse is counterintuitive to our daily existence. Blue light settings are adjusted to allow for brief weather updates.

*

You can do anything you want. Hard work pays off and meritocracy is a level playing field. Just M A N I F ES T. Don't worry about handcuffs or the acquisition of assets by the super-rich. Take photos of yourself drinking coffee against a bland background, talk about your privately funded business plans.

*

How do you determine what constitutes a wasted life? Lying to your boss about how all along you were just pretending? That you mistook models of financial gain for a highly ironic theatrical script? I had a life and lost it all by talking to the wrong people about how we should regenerate coral reefs.

*

In a bid to release funds, I remortgaged my nervous system. The bank provided a free-post envelope for me to send it in. It came out easy enough; a fat worm yanked by a beak. I can get it back in thirty years and legally it has to be refrigerated. I'm not sure how I'll live like this, but then does anyone?

*

I knew it was coming to an end and so I prepared. I had a call with a secret agent. They infected my inner ear with a mind control device. It spread throughout my cells until I turned into a drone. They flew me into a recruitment fair and exploded my intestines all over their new polyester suits.

*

Although sleep was fleeting, the night became full of dreams. I saw a huge cloud of bats rear up and destroy a city. I saw a laser beam from deep inside space cut the earth clean into two. I would wake up shouting, covered in sweat. Daytime was a numbness of coffee and benign action items.

*

It was always before meetings that my auditory bones would morph into a beetle. It crawled from my ear and walked across my to-do list. The wax on its feet scrawled words about the dangers of cortisol exposure, and how short our lives are. I ignored it, right until it jumped into my lap.

*

This mad person covered themselves in flour and salt and bundled themselves into an oven. When they had risen, they walked into town and sat down on the floor. They allowed strangers to snap off and eat an arm, a finger. Not godliness, just a vital communal interest, a vision of future states.

*

Reverse construction companies began to spring up all over. They would downsize skyscrapers and offer seminars on rewilding urban areas. They were taken to court by a man that owned the patent for water, said that it would kill his business. Apparently, he was hit by a recycling truck.

*

As food became more expensive, politicians decided to float the idea of creating lab grown food from the homeless. They went on tv to demonstrate the science. When they gave their samples, a burning portal opened beneath their feet. It consumed them before belching them out, a pulsating heap of flesh.

*

Like cigarettes, all ATM cards had to carry a health warning. In the lobbies of financial institutions, they had to hang pictures of the damage that money does to the human mind. One showed a man with an open shotgun wound. Another showed a child suffocating inside a substandard private let.

*

They rounded up anyone with access to climate data and forced them to have cosmetic surgery. To prove that rising ocean temperatures are a *good* thing they pushed them into a cauldron and lit a fire. The footage was broadcast on all right-wing networks. Such smiles as the water bubbled.

*

We shy away from violence, but honestly, it's just dormant. Before the oil in the pine needles paint the roof orange, we will have to relent. Embody rage, embody the subjugated, embody lunatic dolphins, embody the de-magnetization of the poles. Conditioned apathy has no calorific content.

*

I awoke wanting to know my future. With dependency upon planetary alignment, I focused on the ascension of Mars, held my hands to the sky. Nothing to be seen but inevitable death and triviality. I laughed quietly and set my alarm. I fell back to sleep and dreamt about locusts, the risen undead.

*

When tradition is obfuscated, large structures no longer nomenclate. You can choose for yourself whether this is a poem, a boat made from paper, or a baseball bat. All I want is to be a feather again, to float above the sirens, the ones that warn of tsunami, eruptions, the magnitude of greed.

*

Hope is a strange thing. It lingers in the palms of acceptance, of holding up the sky in one hand and completing expenses in the other. Ultimately nothing matters until it does. I've repeated this so often that masonry bees always seem to mistake my mouth for cheap vanity renovation projects.

ACKNOWLEDGMENTS

Sincerest thanks to the editors of the following journals and magazines where some of the poetry in this book first appeared: *The87press*, *Finished Creatures*, *Orphic Press*, *Poetry Wales*.

'Apathy Catalogue Exploration' first appeared in *Opening Line: An affordable anthology of contemporary poetry* (2025, Broken Sleep Books)

'Attack Route From East River' first appeared in *Devastation Songs: An anthology of Kaiju writing* (2024, Broken Sleep Books)

Introductory epigraph taken from the film *Wall Street* (1987) directed and co-written by Oliver Stone.

Many thanks to Will Alexander, Fran Lock and Rob Kiely for taking the time to read the book and write some supporting words to accompany it, it is massively appreciated.

I'd also like to thank *Broken Sleep Books,* & Aaron Kent for his unwavering friendship & support. Lots of love to my wife Caroline, my daughter Dorrie, Amanda McPherson, and to my extended family Emma, Rue, & Otis Kennedy. Huge thanks to Dean Rhetoric and Agnieszka Studzińska for their feedback and suggestions along the way. Big love to Tim Brooks and the YOFC…Why Not Us?

LAY OUT YOUR UNREST

www.ingramcontent.com/pod-product-compliance
Lightning Source LLC
Chambersburg PA
CBHW020215090426

42734CB00008B/1076